Ukulele for Beginners

A Beginners Guide and Songbook, to Learn and Play Ukulele Reading different Chords, including Popular Songs

by Andrew Scott

Introduction

Welcome to the personally rewarding world of playing a musical instrument – the UKULELE! Imagine sitting around the campfire or at the beach entertaining friends with singalongs for hours on end. Then again, your passion might lie in only playing for your own enjoyment and accomplishment or playing with other musicians in a Ukulele band.

This is all easily within your grasp as the Ukuleles' learning curve is anything but steep. In no time at all, you should be strumming simple songs and easily recognizable melodies. Anyone from a grandchild to a grandparent (and beyond) can quickly be playing. As there are only four strings and tuning is considered open, that is to say, strumming the instrument without placing your fingers on the fretboard is actually a chord (it is actually an Am7 chord just so you know). How difficult is that after all?

Playing the Ukulele is entertaining and fun not to mention easy to learn. You can't deny the charm of the Ukuleles' happy sound and easily recognizable sweet tone. I must mention one of my favorite artists who plays the Ukulele, Eddie Vedder of Pearl Jam fame, who can argue about playing this little instrument after reading that? He has been quoted as saying "Its an activist instrument." He has even recorded a solo album entitled "Ukulele Songs" which he refers to the Ukulele as an "Instant community builder." Again, who can argue with one of history's most influential musicians regarding The Ukulele? I can't.

The Ukulele is a wonderful instrument to pick up. Maybe you are a guitarist looking for some variety like I was or maybe you have never played an instrument in your life. As with everything, we all have our reasons.

Its soft nylon strings are easier to play than the typical steel strings of the guitar not to mention there are fewer strings. Being a smaller size instrument is an advantage also reducing wrist tension and discomfort because notes and chords easier to reach and form.

Then let's not overlook affordability. Buying a decent Ukulele will not break the bank, rest assured. You can purchase one that will give you years of enjoyment for under $80. And due to its small size, it's the ultimate in portability! Throw it in the back of your car or bring it with you on the plane. Try doing that with a drum set. Plus, its friendly, fun and just sounds great. You can easily adapt almost any song to be played on the Ukulele. I know when I play "Stairway to Heaven" on my Ukulele my friends' mouths will drop open in disbelief. I personally think my uke rendition of that classic sounds better than it does on guitar. I believe it is the subtle sweetness of the instruments' sound.

We will be exploring step by step: the sizes of Ukuleles, choosing the correct beginner model and suggested models with model numbers, identification of the parts, holding the instrument, tuning, correct hand position, the Ukulele notes, reading the chord diagrams, chords, major and minor chords, 7th chords, a flat chord, sample practice exercises and then completing with chord diagram overview of 108 chords.

Keep in mind most songs can be and typically are played with three or four simple chords; Yet from this introductory guide you can continue onwards of possibly even being the next "Tiny Tim" or as I detailed before, Eddie Vedder if you are unfamiliar with the former.

Even though there are plenty of books on this subject on the market, thanks again for choosing this one!

Every effort was made to ensure it is full of as much useful information as possible, please enjoy!

Learning Ukulele is Easy

The ukulele is an easy and simple instrument, yet intensely rewarding to play. Four strings, with many chords and songs being played with one finger. Yes, you read that statement correctly, one finger. And it gets simpler. Strumming the four open strings is a chord (it's an Am7 if you were curious and all this will be explained in detail later in this book).

To make it easier, here are a few of the best tips for those who are just beginning to play Ukulele:

- **Never compromise on price.** We will talk about this more in later chapters. The biggest reason to make sure you are not buying a cheap instrument is the longevity of it. You want something that is going to last and is going to produce the sounds you are looking to create.

- **Start on the right foot.** Do not move too quickly forward. You need to learn about the different parts of the instrument, for example. If you do not know which part does what, or which part is where it will make everything moving forward far easier.

- **Research wood types.** Different types of wood create different sounds. There are low-grade woods, alongside high-grade ones. The more expensive the instrument, the better grade the wood.

- **Keep your eyes on the prize.** Make sure that you watch more experienced musicians playing. Watch their hands, especially as they are making sounds you want to mimic. This is the easiest way to gain experience without an instructor.

- **Exercise your hands.** There are several different exercises which will help your hands get used to the idea of playing. You can expect to have cramps in your hands at first. Doing different exercises will help you reduce the strain.

- **Keep your nails short.** This is especially true for the hand you use for strumming. However, most people are not going to have long nails on one hand and short ones on the other. Your nails will get in the way of being able to strum correctly.

- **Watch videos of you playing. As** with all things, it is easiest to see your mistakes when you are watching yourself do something. Taking videos, especially those focused on your hands, will help you "catch" yourself doing things incorrectly.

As silly as it might sound, make sure you are taking time to appreciate your journey. Do not get caught up in moving forward too quickly. Everything will come in time. Hopefully these tips will come in handy. Just keeping moving forward and refer back to this book whenever you feel like you are hitting a wall in your progression. Now, just how easy is it to learn how to play Ukuleles?

Even easier than learning guitar, as it turns out!

Learning Ukulele is Easier Than Guitar

Building on the previous chapter, let's examine the guitar for a moment and do the math. Guitar = six strings. Ukulele = four strings. Six vs. four. Easier. Strum the four open strings on the Ukulele = actual chord.

Strum the open six strings on a guitar = unrecognizable mess. Within only a day or two, you can be playing very simple songs and melodies using only one finger and, in some instances, no fingers. Only a strum. Not true for the guitar. Also, the typical Ukulele string is nylon/plastic whereas the typical guitar string is steel, ouch!

Here are the main differences between guitars and ukuleles:

- **Less strings, less problems!** As said, a Ukulele has fewer strings than a guitar. Less to learn, but just as much fun to be had!

- **They are incredibly easy to transport.** No matter where you go, you can generally bring your ukulele with you. The smaller sizes, such as the popular soprano, can easily fit in your backpack or a weekender bag.

- **So much less expensive than guitars.** You will not have to put down nearly as much money to start playing Ukulele as you might have to with guitar.

- **A great stepping stone to guitars.** Do you eventually want to start playing guitar? That is totally fine! The lessons you learn with your ukulele will transfer almost perfectly to guitars.

- **A unique, but very popular, sound.** Who does not have a love for the crisp, "plucky" sound that only a ukulele can make? It just always seems to bring joy to people everywhere you go. Guitars are unable to produce that sound.

There are many more reasons, but these are some of my favorites. Enough about guitars, though. Let us jump right into the subject matter of this book- everything you need to know about the ukulele!

Ukulele Sizes/Sizing

For this book, we are concentrating on three sizes of Ukulele. The traditional Soprano, the larger Concert, and the largest size, the Tenor. There is a fourth size, traditionally, but that is the Baritone. There is also a smaller size than the Soprano, which is called the Sopranissimo. It is the teensy, tiny, little Ukulele that you may be the most used to seeing. It has gained wild popularity in the mainstream eye.

However, it is not a realistic starting point. For reference, these are the sizes by measurement:

- **Sopranissimo:** 16in / 40cm

- **Soprano:** 20in / 51cm

- **Concert:** 23in / 58cm

- **Tenor:** 26in / 66cm

- **Baritone:** 30in / 76cm

As you can see, there are quite a few differences in sizing. The largest, the Baritone, is nearly double in size from the smallest, the Sopranissimo. It is a perfect gradient of sizes and pretty easy to find one which is perfect for you.

Again, for the purposes of this book, I will only be referencing the middle three sizes as they are the most relevant.

Below you will see the three sizes we will be referencing.

The major difference is that the first three all follow the same style of tuning. The Baritone works off of a different style, and so it is absolutely beyond a beginner's ability or knowledge. The standard tuning is G-C-E-A. We will go over that in a later chapter, as well as how to remember the tuning.

Making sure that you have a correctly sized instrument for yourself is absolutely crucial to your success in learning how to play the Ukulele. As you can see below, there are several differences between a Ukulele which is the proper size for the person, and one which is too large.

A smaller Ukulele will allow you to easily reach around to strum different chords. A k

It is important to note that many students will progress upwards in stages. Not just in ability, but also in Ukulele sizes. The smallest, the Soprano, is generally used to begin with. The tiny stature of the Soprano makes it easy to reach the strings and learn how to position it in relation to your body.

Next in this series of upgrades is the Concert. While larger than the Soprano by quite a bit, it is still smaller than the largest size of Ukulele that I will be talking about. The Concert is a lovely step in the right direction for those students who are ready to advance. Children, or very small adults, will most likely not move upwards due to their inability to properly use a larger instrument. As mentioned, the Ukulele must be a proper size for however is playing it.

The Tenor is the largest. Whichever you decide to begin with, remember to buy a quality instrument and not a plastic toy you will quickly become discouraged with. Plan on spending $50 to $80 for a suitable introductory model.

Ukulele Tuning

The standard tuning for a Ukulele is **G-C-E-A**. I use simple sayings to remember the notes. There are multiple different acronyms you can use! Here are a couple of them that are pretty popular:

- **G**ood **C**ows **E**at **A**lways or **G**et **C**razy **E**very **A**fternoon.

- **G**otta **C**atch 'Em **A**ll

- **G**od **C**reated **E**verything **A**men

- **G**ravity **C**auses **E**arthly **A**ttraction

Whatever mnemonic device you use to remember the standard tuning, just make sure you do, in fact, remember. It can take some time to get it down, but these little sayings help a whole lot.

There are a few different ways in which you can tune a Ukulele. You can do so on your own, the "traditional way", or you can get a little help in the matter. There are two ways to do this.

Apps exist that you can download to your phone. These are popular, and many of them happen to be free of charge. Although, it is always important to remember that you always get what you pay for. Sometimes it is easier to just pay a little bit of money to get something that is going to work out easier for you.

You can also invest in a digital Ukulele tuner. This is going to be the most accurate way to tune your ukulele. You can find them at any number of retailers, or even online if you do not want to leave the house. These are available for under $20 for the most part.

Suggested Selection of Beginner Ukuleles

Now, which one is right for you? Great question! The world of music is vast, and can be confusing if you are not familiar with instruments in general. Ukuleles are a great place to start! They are generally less confusing than other instruments and very friendly for those who are just beginning as a result. Many people who play the Ukulele choose to learn right on their own.

There are several sizes, as I spoke about a couple of chapters prior. Of course, each Ukulele varies from brand to brand. Just as with anything else you have brands which are "favored" and ones which you will be warned to stay away from. I am going to help you skip the trouble by giving you the best recommendations for each size. You will have to try them out and see which one you like best, and which one is easiest. As always, I do suggest starting out with a Soprano and moving forward as you need to.

These are the Ukulele models which I recommend for each size:

- **Kala KA-15S (Soprano size):** The Soprano size is recommended for all beginners. The small build allows for you to more easily manipulate the strings and find the correct placement for your hands. It will also allow you to stretch out your fingers so that the larger sizes will not cause as much cramping as you use them. All beginners will start on a Soprano, generally speaking. This is also, notably, the most "traditional" size. When you imagine the sound that a Ukulele makes, this is the one.

- **Donner DUC-1 (Concert size):** This is the next size up from the Soprano. The concert is a good starting place if you have hands which are just too large to properly strum a Soprano. This size has a light, "plucky" tone, much like the Soprano. However, it also has a touch of something deeper in it's tone which pulls more towards the larger Tenor size.

- **Lohanu LU-T (Tenor size):** Tenor sizes have become increasingly popular in the last few years. They are highly versatile and can be used for a variety of purposes. Many people love the deep, hollow sound they produce, and find it more elegant than the traditional Ukulele sound. The Tenor is also a much better match for anybody who is using their fingers to strum instead of a pick.

Even though it may seem tempting, you do not want to waste your time on a cheap Ukulele. The old saying is true- you get what you pay for. A cheap model is not going to bring you the results you want, and it will not help you learn to play properly. The sounds will be off, and it will wear out quickly. Do not waste your time with some cheap, plastic toy you will become frustrated with.

The suggested models listed above range in price from about $50 to $80. This may seem expensive, yes, but it is well worth the investment. Between the three you should be able to find exactly what you are looking for.

The Parts of a Ukulele

Now that we have covered some of the basics, it is time to start understanding different parts of this instrument. After all, instructions will not do you much good if you do not know what they are even referring to in the first place. While this is certainly not an in-depth explanation, it is a great point to start at. You will not need to know the inner workings until you have gotten a little further on your path to Ukulele bliss!

We will start at the top of the instrument and work our way down:

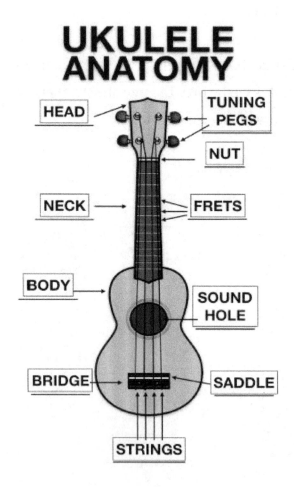

- **Tuning Pegs:** If you need to tune your Ukulele, this is going to be the place you do so. There are several different names which can refer to this part. Tuning keys is one, as is machine heads (not just a plural of the famous band, as it turns out).

- **Headstock:** The top-most part of the Ukulele. The headstock, also known simply as "the head", is where everything attaches to. The tuning pegs, for example, are found here. Most brands will slap their logo on this part, traditionally speaking. You may also be able to find the identifying code, the serial number, which matches that specific model.

- **Nut:** This part is complimentary to the bridge. The nut helps to keep the strings secured in place so that they do not fall out of position. It is a small, but essential, part of the instrument.

- **Frets:** Metal bars which are on the fretboard.

- **Fretboard:** The little boards which the frets are placed upon.

- **Neck:** The long, skinny part which goes between the head and body. All of these names make it pretty easy to remember which parts are where. This is where all of the frets are.

- **Soundhole:** As you can probably imagine, this is that circle which is cut out of the center of the body, on the front of the Ukulele. The soundhole is the mode through which the vibrations can escape. The vibrations, of course, are responsible for the noise that you hear! Physics is the language of music.

- **Body:** This is the "bottom" section of the Ukulele. It consists of a hollowed middle surrounded by special sized and carved wood. The body is where all of the magic (physics) happen and is responsible for the creation of noise. Depending on the type of wood, you will have a different sound. This is the reason why making sure you look into the different woods and what they do is so important.

- **Strings:** These are, of course, what you are strumming to transfer vibrations! Most people know what the strings are. They are pretty self-explanatory.

- **Bridge:** A thin bar which is at almost the very bottom of the instrument. It sits on top of a large bar, and both of these parts help to keep all of the strings in place and tight.

Correct Positions Sitting and Standing

So, now that we have covered the bases as far as terminology and perks go, I am going to teach you how to properly hold a ukulele. There is some technique involved here but it is very easy to catch onto. I highly suggest that you also watch videos on the subject, as incorporating a live-action version of directions can help you immensely.

It is important to keep in mind that incorrect positioning or posture, in most cases, will not cause harm to your instrument. It will just make it harder on you as a musician. You need to make sure that you are using your Ukulele properly in order to learn how to play correctly.

There are differences between all the sizes, as well. For the larger models you may choose to sit down while you play. This tends to be the most comfortable way, since the larger sizes are almost as big as a guitar. You can hold it on your leg if you choose to sit down while you play.

Here is a few general rules of thumbs as far as proper holding goes:

- Keep your arms bare. The way that you hold the ukulele is dependent on the friction between the soundboard and your arm holds it in place.

- Your thumb should always remain behind the ukulele's neck.

- Your fingers should always be held parallel to the frets.

- Keep yourself relaxed through it. Tension in your body will affect the way that you play and the sounds produced.

- If you are sitting down, never allow the ukulele to "slouch" down into your lap. This causes excessive strain your wrist, which in turn can cause a lot of damage.

- Keep your elbow close to your body and not bend outwards. However, do not keep your arm flat against yourself, either. Happy medium!

So, now that we have gone over a few things to keep in mind, I am now going to lay out exactly how to hold the instrument.

First, you are going to hold it against your upper stomach (diaphragm). Keep your right forearm bent gently and at a ninety-degree angle to the soundhole. This will allow you to strum to your heart's content with your right hand. You should have enough freedom of movement to move up and down the part of the neck which is attached to the body of the ukulele.

Make sure that your strumming hand does not fall down towards the bridge. This is going to affect the sound negatively as it is below the soundhole. Naturally, that will make it produce different sounds. It just does not sound great.

Now, I am going to talk about what you will be doing with your left arm. This is also known as your "fretting" arm. It is the one which is going to be holding down different frets while your other hand strums.

Place the pad, the fleshy part, of your thumb above the nut. If you forget what any of these parts are, please reference the explanation and diagram from earlier. Now, you should also be underneath the third fret, so try to stay in between there and the nut. This will, of course be on the back of the head. Your fingers will come "under" the neck and be pointing up onto the frets.

To keep from hurting yourself make sure you keep your wrist and arm as straight as possible. You will have to move a little to reach different chords. However, as a general rule, keep them level. It takes a lot of strain out of your wrist!

Below, I have placed some photos for reference. You can have a much better idea of how to play whether you are standing up or sitting.

Correct Position Standing

Correct Position Sitting

Finger Chart

Refer to the diagram below for finger identification.

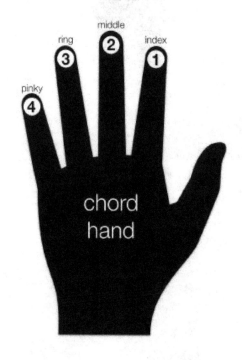

HOW TO
READ A CHORD CHART

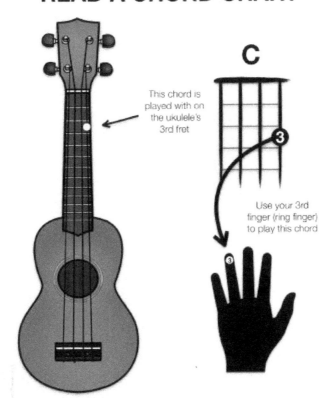

As shown in the hand pictorial above, the T indicates the Thumb, the number 1 corresponds to the index finger, the number 2 corresponds to the middle finger, the number 3 corresponds to the ring finger and the number 4 corresponds to the pinky finger.

Use the numbers when reading the chord charts discussed later. Although the diagram above shows a left hand the hand layout is obviously identical for your right hand.

Ukulele Fretboard Chart

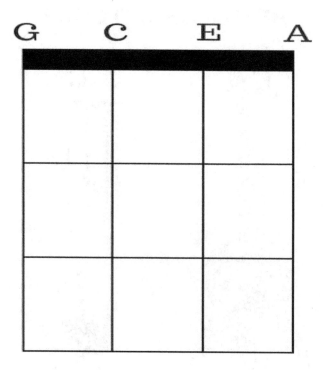

Refer to the fret board chart above for an understanding of the Ukulele chord chart. When reading Ukulele chord charts, the vertical lines correspond to the strings on the fret board. Think of these as a visual representation with the G string closest to your body. Keep in mind the G string is also known as the 4th string, the C string is also known as the 3rd string, the E string is also known as 2nd string and the A string is also known as the 1st string. A fret board chart is also known as Tablature or "Tab."

Please note: There are alternate tunings, but for the purposes of this book we will only be concentrating on the typical G-C-E-A tuning.

Correct Hand Position

Proper hand position is absolutely crucial while you are learning how to play any instrument. It is no secret that arthritis tends to be prevalent in artists and especially musicians. I am not saying this to scare you off, of course. I just want to make sure you understand that preventing these injuries is very important.

If you follow my instructions you should not have any issues in this regard, however. Just remember to stretch your fingers and keep your positioning correct.

For your fretting hand, the left one, you will be resting the neck between your thumb and pointer finger. Keep it nestled there so that it is steady and secure. This should not cause too much tension in your hand. Your fingers should be able to reach chords easily from this position. You want the pad of your thumb, as mentioned prior, to rest between the nut and roughly the third fret.

As for the right hand, your strumming hand, you will want to figure out the best way to strum for you personally. There are several different styles! We will talk about the "regular" way to do so, however, since that will be the easiest for a beginner. As you move forward through your musical journey you may find other ways you like more, however.

You want your hand to be towards the middle of the soundhole. Your arm should be level, as well, with only a slightly bent elbow. Do not let your elbow go too far "out" as this causes strain. Conversely, do not keep it too close to your body because this will cause it to be less secure.

Using a pick may be the easiest way for a beginner to

You may be wondering whether there is a special style of ukulele for left-handed players. There actually is not! You can use a ukulele either way- it is really up to you. Some people who are left-handed still choose to strum with their right hand. Some who write with their right hand will use their left to strum. You just have to figure out which way is most comfortable for you.

However, it is generally recommended that you play right-handed first. You are, technically speaking, holding the ukulele backwards when you use your left hand to strum. There are a couple of different ways to tackle this. You could either re-string your ukulele, which can be tricky, or you could play it backwards.

Learning how to string a ukulele gives you a great tool which expands your musical horizons. However, it can be quite a bit of effort. You can always go into your local music store and see if anybody there can help you. Keep in mind that if you go this route you will not be able to play another ukulele. The re-strung ukulele will be tuned different than all of the others.

If you play it backwards, you are just going to have to commit the new order of strings to memory. Everything will be upside down compared to the books you will be reading music out of. It takes a little bit of practice and thought, but you can definitely get it down pat after a while.

Refer to the pictures and descriptions below for an understanding of the correct hand position.

Strumming the Ukulele

Strumming your Ukulele is one of the first things that you are going to learn, naturally. There are several different ways to do this. It really comes down to how you feel and what way works best for you. However, I am going to keep things simple today and just teach you to the most universal way of doing things.

You can go one of two ways: using a pick, or just using your bare fingers. Note that using a pick at first is not recommended, although it may save your fingers some pain. It can be more difficult to use a pick because of how precise you have to be with it. Using your fingers allows you to really get a feel for the strings and how everything works. It is also easier to manipulate them when you use your bare fingers.

The bottom of your thumb, the fleshy part, is going to be one of the main focus points of your strumming. You can use the bare, fleshy bottom of your thumb, as well as the bottom of your index finger. You will also be using the back of your index finger's nail. So, it will be the bottom of those two fingers, as well as the back of their nails, and the front of their nails. If you so choose, you can even incorporate the usage of all of your fingers, as well as the back of your fingernails.

Eventually, you are going to want to try out different patterns and ways of playing. For now, try to focus mainly on that thumb and index finger.

Another method is to alternate between using your thumb, and then either your finger or thumbnail for another strumming pattern. All the methods I have described thus far can be referred to as finger style.

The second method is using a plectrum or "pick." Hold the pick somewhat loosely in your fingers. This will require some practice until you get a good feel for how to do so. Take your time and do not be discouraged if you are not able to figure it out at first. You will be holding the pick between your thumb and pointer finger. Of course, those are normally the two fingers responsible for your strumming (for the most part).

Be careful about how you apply pressure with a pick. One of the reasons that it is not recommended for beginners is the danger of breaking one of your strings. This will require you to either restring the ukulele yourself or bring it into a shop. Repair costs are not expensive, but it can certainly be a damper on your day. There is also the time spent bringing it in to be restrung. And, of course, in the meantime you will not be able to play.

There are some serious benefits to using a pick, however. For example, using a pick can better allow you to achieve that beautiful island-esque sound the Ukulele is known for. It is hard to get those same crisp notes while using only your fingers. You have to weigh the risk and reward and figure out if you would like to begin with a pick or your fingers.

Two down strums with one up strum repeating with many, many variations on this. Three down strums with two up strums. The possibilities are virtually endless, honestly. As you become more and more confident with your playing you will begin to understand just how many opportunities are available to you.

Note: It is recommended to not use a pick at first and use the back/top of your pointer finger.

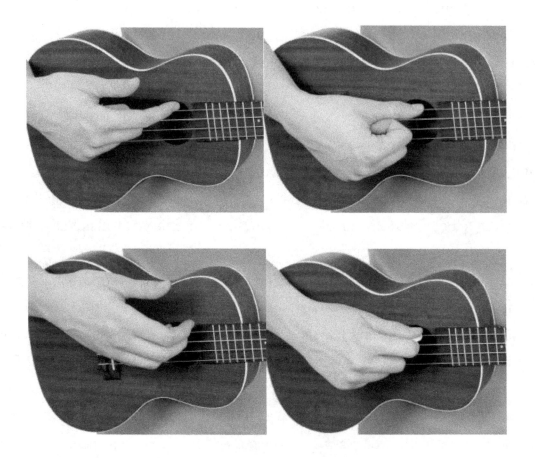

How to hold a pick

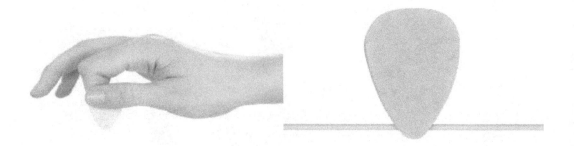

Ukulele Fretboard Note Diagram

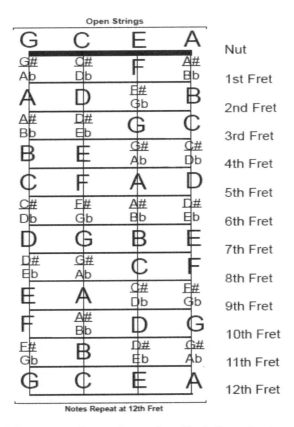

Refer to the fingerboard diagram above for a detailed description. The horizontal lines refer to the frets whereas the vertical lines refer to the strings. There are 12 frets corresponding to the 12 notes and then repeat starting at the 13th fret. Notice the strings are labeled G-C-E-A.

Look at the G string 5th fret C. The note is the same as the next string C. Then look at the C string at the 4th fret, E. This note is the same as the next string E. Then look at the E string 5th fret, A. This note is the same as the next string A. Possibly you have figured out you can check to se if you are in tune using this method. Fascinating right? I promise this is only the beginning.

When referring to a note to be made using your finger on the fret board, it will show the number of the finger to be used. 1-2-3-4 and we have previously referred to the number and corresponding finger.

Ukulele Chord

Ukulele Chord Definition

There must be at least three notes played in order for it to be considered a chord. You can also refer to three chords as a triad. They are all played at the same time. There are many different chords you can play on the ukulele- and they are all far easier than they would be on a guitar. Chords also tend to sound better since the ukulele is not nearly as complex.

All songs are based off of chords. When you start to build off of chords and play them back to back in different ways, you are officially on your way to making real music. Chords are not all meant to be played at the same time, however. They are vastly complex and must be placed purposefully. When you are playing around you will figure out pretty quickly which chords sound great together and which ones make you grit your teeth. It is just about experimentation- you will figure it out as you go!

Note the same chord can and will be found in many areas of the fretboard there are different ways to finger the same chords. This is advantageous, however! When you start building sounds on top of each other you may want to create a chord one way so that it is easier for you to move your fingers into position for the next one. It is important to learn how to make the same sound using different areas on your fretboard.

Ukulele Chord Concept

Have you ever heard of a chord tone? Most likely, you have not. This is a pretty basic concept in musical theory but if you have never had formal training in the musical arts you may be a little undereducated in that regard.

You can think of chord tones as the stepping stones to actual chords. They are the building blocks which make up all of the chords you will play. Let us talk about a few terms you may be unfamiliar with.

- **Chord Tone:** The building blocks of all chords. You will learn how to play different tones before you start building into chords.

- **Chords:** At least three notes played at the same time. They sound harmonious together. I have placed a wonderful diagram in the last chapter so that you can practice different chords. You will want to master these before you move on to more complex sounds and music.

- **The Root:** As you can imagine, this is the "root" of the sound. It is the note which is considered the strongest one in the sound. A power chord is compromised of only a root and a fifth.

- **The Third:** This is responsible for making a sound either "high" or "low". You can also think of it as a "happy" sound or a "sad" sound.

- **The Fifth:** In order to pack a punch with your sounds, you need to rely on the fifth. You have probably heard this word before but did not know what it meant. Power chords are made by playing only two of the chord tones. These two are the root, and the fifth.

- **Major Chord:** The first style of chord you will learn how to play. The major chord is often thought to be the most important one in music, as well. It is very important!

- **Minor Chord:** A chord which is only comprised of a root, a perfect fifth, as well as a minor third. They are harder to play and require a more trained ear.

As previously noted, a chord is a minimum of three notes which is known as a triad. These notes can be a combination of fretted notes and open notes.

There are several different reasons why you may want to use open notes. Most people who play will choose to play fretted notes. There is some strange bias against open notes! However, the decision really comes down to both sound as well as the playability you are able to achieve.

The defining factor in open notes is that they sound much "brighter" than fretted notes. They also last quite a bit longer. You have to be careful where you place the open notes, however, because they will outshine the fretted notes. It can sound awful if they are completely overtaking the chords!

With an open note, you need to actively stop the note from playing. This means pressing down on the string to make it stop. Naturally, open notes are, in most cases, considered harder to play. This is part of the reason that most people end up avoiding them altogether. You cannot keep avoiding them as you make your way further into your journey through music, however.

Fretted notes can be stopped just by releasing on the fret enough that the note ends. You will need to try playing both ways before you figure out which works best for you.

Reading a Ukulele Chord Diagram

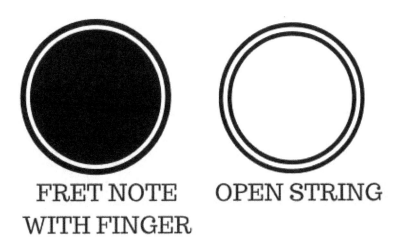

FRET NOTE
WITH FINGER

OPEN STRING

As shown above in the pictorial, a black dot signifies placing your finger on the string/fret (a number will be in the circle indicating the corresponding finger to be used) and a white dot indicates playing an open string.

Ukulele Chord Symbols

The chord symbols are typically shown at the top or bottom of the chord chart. These are an "X" which indicates the string is not to be played and an "O" which indicates the string is to be played open. It really can't get much easier than that. Remember I have said before the Ukulele is easy and fun to learn and play.

Understanding MAJOR and minor Symbols

When discussing major and minor chords without going into too music theory, just remember when you see a capital "M" (or without anything after the chord letter assume it is a major) it is referring to a Major chord and when referring to a minor chord it is a lower case "m". For example, a GM or G indicates a G Major and Gm indicates G minor. Simple again, right?

Beginner Chord Chart Overview

Use the diagram below to play different chords. You will want to practice these over and over again until you really begin to understand how to play them. These are the building blocks which will lead to both being able to play more complex music, but also to begin writing it yourself.

If you want to become more advanced, then this is a chart you want to pour over every day. Luckily for you, this book can go everywhere with you! That means that the chart, and other handy diagrams, are never too far out of reach.

There are, of course, far more chords than just these ones. Eventually you will master these and want to move on to more advanced chords. This is just the starting point that I think would be best suited to you.

Anyway, here are all of the chords you need to learn how to play first. Have fun, enjoy your ukulele, and keep the music alive!

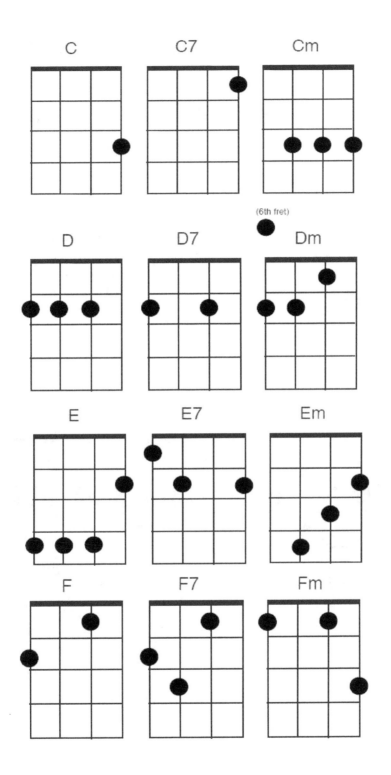

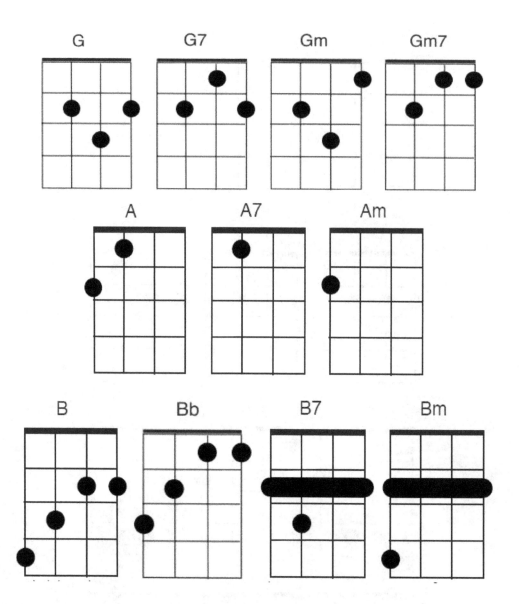

Well, now you have everything you need, hopefully, to be well on your way to making music. The ukulele is one of the most rewarding instruments that you can play. It is simple, has a beautiful sound, and brings endless joy to anybody who hears it. Whether you want to start playing guitar afterward, you want to join a band, or you are just doing it for yourself, the ukulele is such a worthwhile investment. I wish you every bit of luck in your progression. However, after reading my book I do not think that you will need it.

The Easiest Ukulele Chords to Learn to Play

Now is what you have been anxiously awaiting! In the next chapters we will explore in detail how to form each chord. Remember when forming each chord first pluck each string (unless there is an "X" below or above the string which indicates that string is to be muted) individually to ensure it rings out and is not muted by insufficient string pressure or your finger is touching an adjacent open string and muting it.

Now, we are going to get right into learning exactly how you play the Ukulele.

The C Major Chord

Let's start with the easiest chord to form. Here is our first chord we will learn, C Major. As depicted in the diagram below, use your 3rd finger (ring finger) and place it on the 3rd fret of the 1st string, the A string. Use firm pressure to form this chord but do not a death grip. Do not squeeze too tightly likewise and do not hold it too loosely. Pluck each string to verify each string rings out clearly and that none are muted. Readjust your finger position or increase or decrease your finger pressure as necessary until each note rings out clearly.

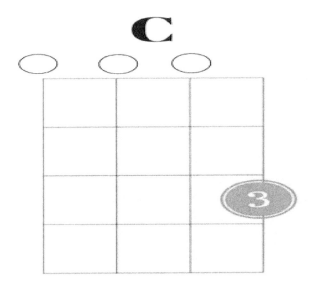

Note: You might be thinking "Why not just use my first finger as that seems easier?" You would be right if you were only going to play a C Major chord all day, but I doubt that is the only thing you want to play on your Ukulele. You want to learn correct hand position from the start and not pick up any bad habits. The primary reason we use the ring finger is we will be forming other chords from this position. You will understand this more clearly as we get into the more difficult chords. Do not try to take any short cuts starting out or it will only hinder your playing later.

Let's understand what it means when you see or play a major chord. A major chords' sound is typically described as happy sounding.

In music theory, the major chord has a root, a major 3rd and a perfect 5th.

The Cm minor Chord

Now let's tackle a more difficult chord, the Cm. Place your pinky finger on the 3rd fret of the A string, place your ring finger on the 3rd fret of E string and then place your middle finger on the 3rd fret of the C string. I know this is tight and difficult but give it a try varying string pressure plucking each string ensuring each string rings out and that none are muted. Do not get frustrated with your second chord as this one is not used often and after you progress you can barre (using one finger across and pressing down multiple strings) this chord with your ring finger.

Some insight into the understanding of the minor chords: minor chords' sounds are considered softer and almost sweeter. Then again, some people describe a minor chord as almost a sad or a moody sound.

In music theory, a minor chord has a root, a minor 3rd and a perfect 5th.

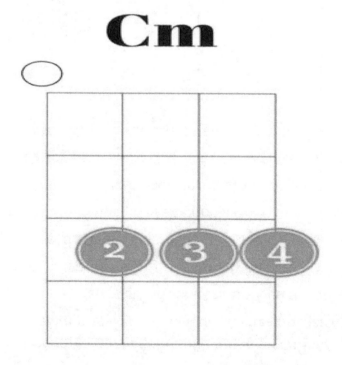

Cm

The C7 Chord

The C7 chord is easy like the C Major chord. Use your index finger on the 1st fret of the A string. Pluck each string ensuring nothing is muted and each string rings out. Modify your finger pressure and placement until you accomplish this.
The 7th chords are typically described as sounding jazzy or bluesy.

In music theory 7th chords are formed with a root, major 3rd, a perfect 5th and a minor 7th note.

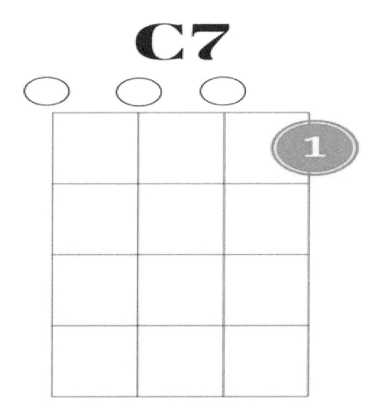

The A Chord

To play the A chord place your index finger on the 1st fret of the C string and your middle finger on the 2nd fret of G string ensuring each string ring out clearly. Modify your finger pressure and placement until you accomplish this.

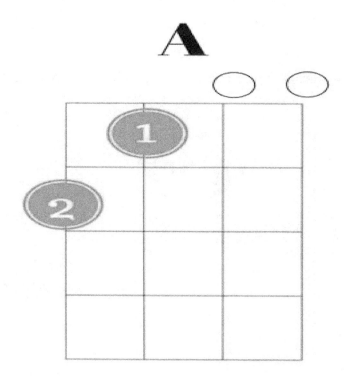

The A minor Chord

To play the Am chord place your middle finger on the 2nd fret of the C string ensuring each string rings out clearly. Modify your finger pressure and placement until you accomplish this.

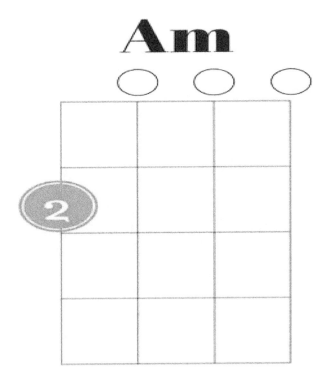

The A7 Chord

To play the A7 chord place your index finger on the 1st fret of the C string ensuring each string rings out clearly. Modify your finger pressure and placement until you accomplish this.

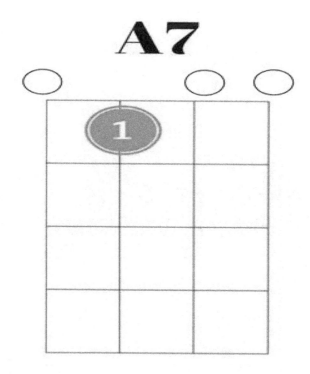

The D Chord

To play the D chord place your index finger on the 2nd fret of the G string, your middle finger on the 2nd fret of the C string and your ring finger on the 2nd fret of the E string ensuring each string rings out clearly. Modify your finger pressure and placement until you accomplish this. This is a difficult chord and do not be discouraged as this one requires a lot of practice and is used often in many songs. I will admit in some songs I will barre this chord with my thumb.

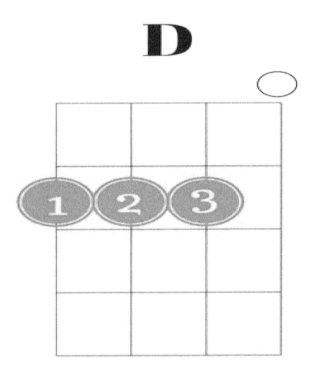

The F Chord

To play the F chord place your index finger on the 1st fret of the E string and your middle finger on the 2nd fret of the G string ensuring each string rings out clearly. Modify your finger pressure and placement until you accomplish this. Notice the "O" above the C and A strings? Remember this indicates they are to be played open.

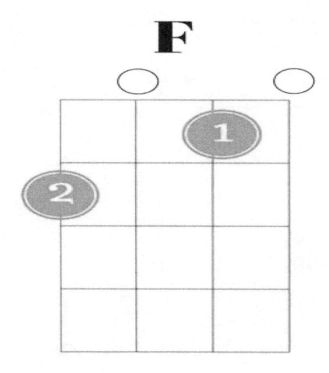

The Fm minor Chord

I will tell you upfront the Fm is difficult but not impossible to master. To play the Fm chord place your index finger on the 1st fret of the G string, your middle finger on the 1st fret of the E string and your pinky on the 3rd fret of the A string ensuring each string rings out clearly. Modify your finger pressure and placement until you accomplish this. This is a tough one but with practice I know you can do it.

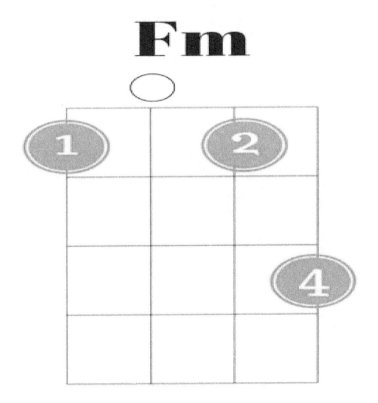

The Dm minor Chord

Place your index finger on the 1st fret of the E string, your middle finger on the 2nd fret of the G string and your ring finger on the 2nd fret of the C string ensuring each string rings out clearly. Modify your finger pressure and placement until you accomplish this. Notice the A string is open and be careful not to mute it.

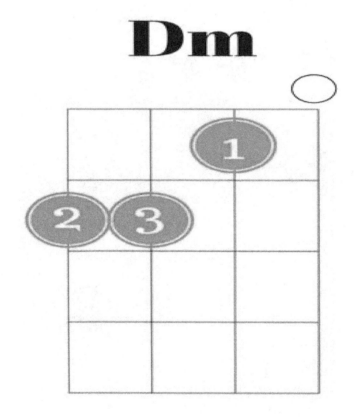

The G Chord

To form a G chord, place your index finger on the 2nd fret of the C string, your middle finger on the 2nd fret of the A string and your ring finger on the 3rd fret of the E string ensuring each string rings out clearly. Modify your finger pressure and placement until you accomplish this. Notice the G string is open and be careful not to mute it.

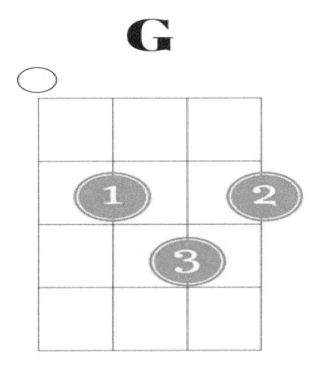

The B Chord

The B chord is a little challenging as it employs a partial barre as we have discussed earlier.

Place your index finger across the E and A strings at the 2nd fret, your middle finger on the 3rd fret of the C string and your ring finger on the 4th fret of the G string ensuring each string rings out clearly. Modify your finger pressure and placement until you accomplish this.

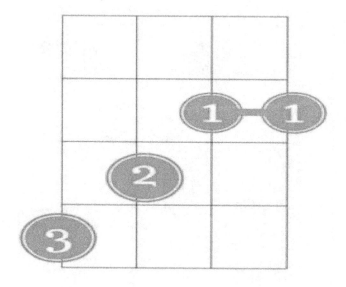

The B♭ flat Chord

Once you have mastered the B chord The B flat chord is simple as it is down a half step in musical terms, you move the entire chord down one fret on the neck towards the nut/tuners.

To play the B flat chord, use your index finger to again barre the E and A strings at the 1st fret, put your middle finger at the 2nd fret of the C string and put your ring finger on the 3rd fret of the G string ensuring each string rings out clearly. Modify your finger pressure and placement until you accomplish this.

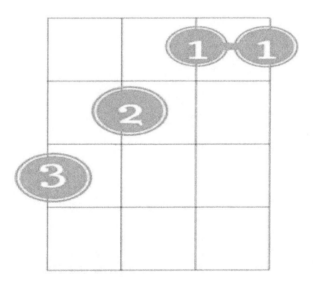

The Gm7

After you have mastered the B chord and the B flat chord the Gm7 chord is even easier as we will see.

To play the Gm7 chord E and A strings at the 1st fret, put your middle finger at the 2nd fret of the C string ensuring each string rings out clearly. Modify your finger pressure and placement until you accomplish this.

Did you notice the difference? It's the same as the B flat without the ring finger on G string.

Gm7

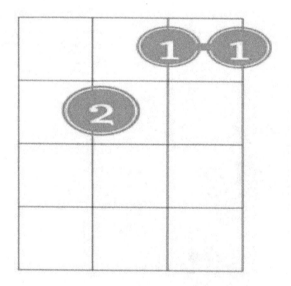

The E Chord with Variations

The E chord is difficult regardless of which variation you use. The first version is a simpler and then the traditional E chord is presented. Doing stretch exercises over time will help with your flexibility and practice, practice, practice.

To make the simplified E chord, put your index finger on the 1st fret of the G string, middle finger on the 2nd fret of A string and put your ring finger on the 4th fret of the C string being sure to leave the E string open and ensuring each string rings out clearly. Modify your finger pressure and placement until you accomplish this.

To play the traditional E chord place your index finger on the 2nd fret of the A string, place your middle finger across the 4th fret of the G, C, and E strings in a barre while simultaneously not muting the A string ensuring each string rings out clearly. Modify your finger pressure and placement until you accomplish this. Notice the E string is open and be careful not to mute it.

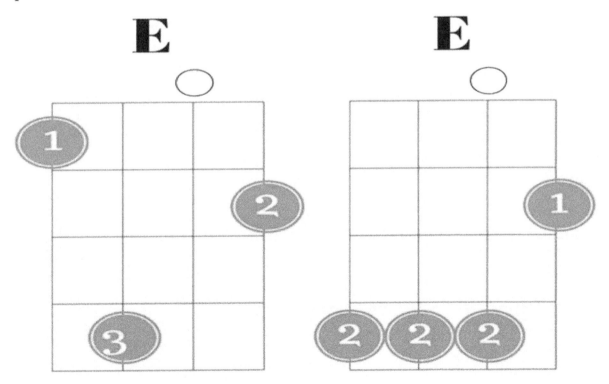

The Bm minor Chord

To form the Bm chord use your index finger to barre the 2nd fret of the C. E and A strings, then place your ring finger on the 4th fret of the G string ensuring each string rings out clearly. Modify your finger pressure and placement until you accomplish this.

Bm

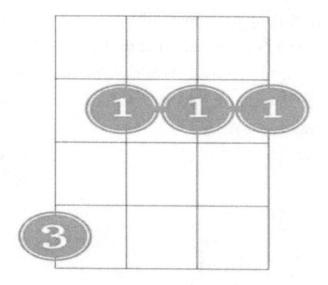

The Em minor Chord

To form the Em chord place your index finger on the 2nd fret of the A string, place your middle finger on the 3rd fret of the E string and then place your ring finger on the 4th fret of the C string ensuring each string rings out clearly. Modify your finger pressure and placement until you accomplish this. Notice the open G string is not muted.

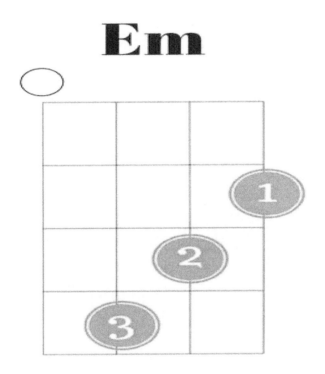

The Gm minor Chord

To form the Gm chord, place your index finger on the 1st fret of the A string, place your ring finger on the 3rd fret of the E string and place your middle finger on the 2nd fret of the C string ensuring each string rings out clearly. Modify your finger pressure and placement until you accomplish this. Notice the G string is open and not to mute it.

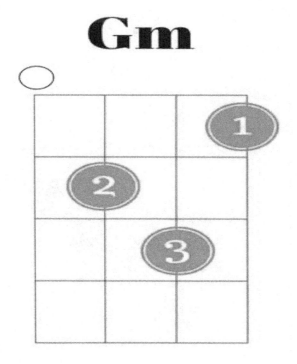

The B7 Chord

To form the B7 chord place your index finger across the entire 2nd fret of all the strings in a "grand" barre (grand barre refers to using a single finger to press all strings down onto the fret board simultaneously) fashion and then place your middle finger on the 3rd fret of the C string ensuring each string rings out clearly. Modify your finger pressure and placement until you accomplish this.

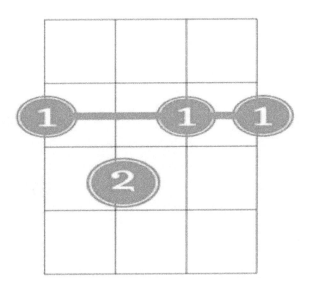

The D7 Chord

To form the D7 chord place your index finger across the entire 2nd fret in the "grand" barre fashion and then place your middle finger on the 3rd fret of the A string ensuring each string rings out clearly. Modify your finger pressure and placement until you accomplish this.

D7

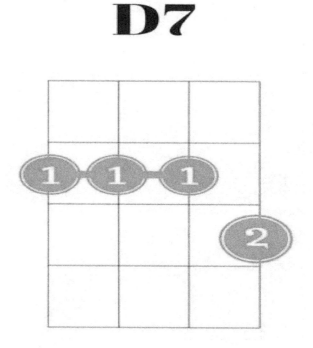

The E7 Chord

To form the E7 chord place your index finger on the first fret of the G string, place your middle finger on the second ret of the C string and place your ring finger of the 2nd fret of the A string ensuring each string rings out clearly. Modify your finger pressure and placement until you accomplish this. Notice the E string is open and be careful not to mute it.

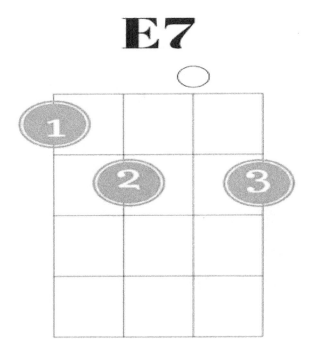

The F7 Chord

To form the F7 chord place your index finger on the 1st fret of the E string, place your middle finger on the 2nd fret of the G string and place your middle finger on the 3rd fret of the C string ensuring each string rings out clearly. Modify your finger pressure and placement until you accomplish this. Notice the A string is open and be careful to not mute it.

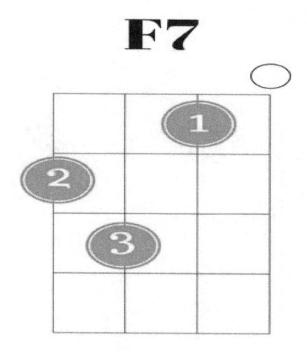

The G7 Chord

To form the G7 chord place your index finger of the 1st fret of the E string, place your middle finger on the 2nd fret of the C string and place your ring finger on the 2nd fret of the A string ensuring each string rings out clearly. Modify your finger pressure and placement until you accomplish this. Ensure you do not mute the G string as it is open.

tough one but with practice I know you can do it

G7

This completes our introduction for forming the most typically used Ukulele chords.

Chord Change Practice Exercise

First Chord Change Practice

Now let's try putting everything together with a simple chord change.

First form a G major chord. Slowly strum four down strokes. Then readjust your fingers to form a C major chord. Slowly strum four down strokes. Repeat three more times and then allow your fingers to rest a couple minutes. Repeat until you feel comfortable with your first chord change practice exercise.

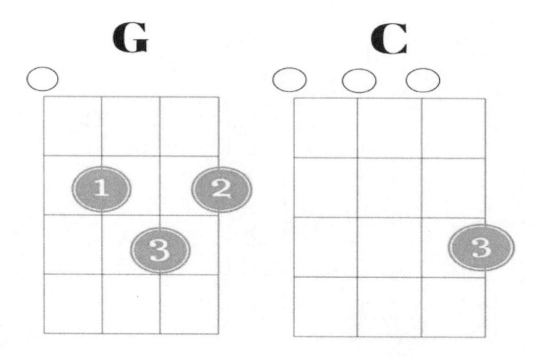

Second Chord Change Practice

Now let's try it again with another simple chord change.

First form a G major chord. Slowly strum four down strokes. Then readjust your fingers to form a F major chord. Slowly strum four down strokes. Repeat three more times and then allow your fingers to rest a couple minutes. Repeat until you feel comfortable with your second chord change practice exercise.

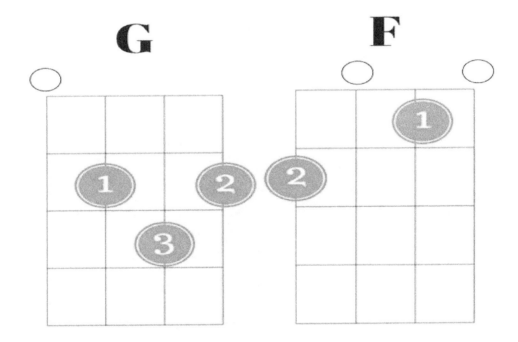

Songbook to Play

Humpty Dumpty

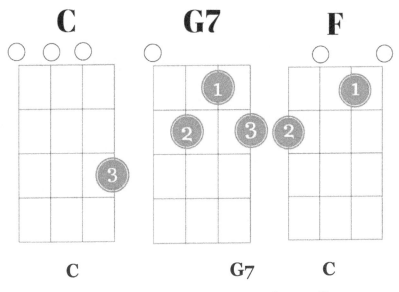

C G7 F

C   G7   C

Humpty Dumpty sat on the wall

C   G7   C

Humpty Dumpty had a great fall

F   C   G7

All the king's horses and all the king's men

F   C   G7   C

Couldn't put Humpty together again

Twinkle Twinkle Little Star

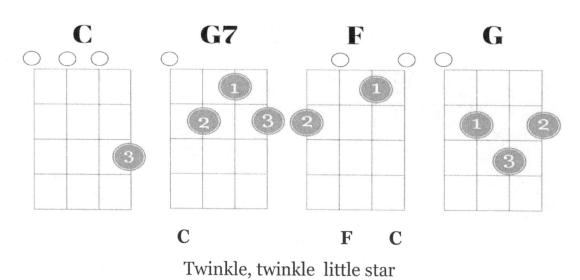

       C   F   C

Twinkle, twinkle little star

   F   C   G7   C

How I wonder what you are

   C   G7   C   G7

Up a-bove the   sky so bright

     C   G7   C G

Like a diamond in the night

  C   F   C

Twinkle, twinkle little star

  F   C   G7   C

How I wonder what you are

Hot Cross Bound

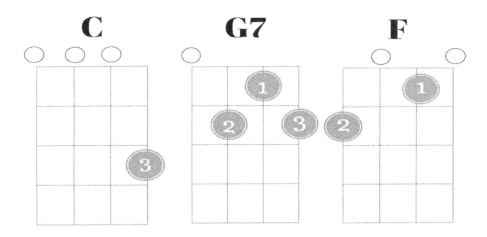

    C   G7   C   C   G7   C

Hot cross buns, hot cross buns

            C   G7

One a penny, two a penny,

   C   G7   C   F

If you have no daughters, Give them to your sons

            C   G7

One a penny, two a penny,

        C G7 C

Hot cross buns

Old Mac Donald had a Farm

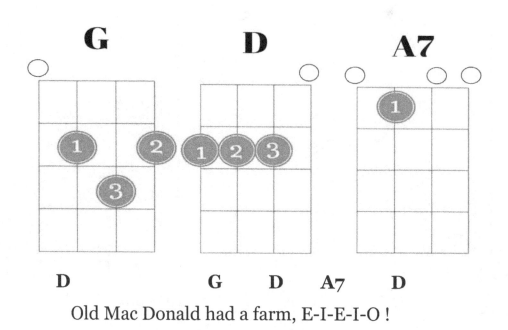

       D   **G**   **D**   **A7**   **D**

Old Mac Donald had a farm, E-I-E-I-O !

       D   **G**   **D**   **A7**   **D**

And on his farm he had some chicks, E-I-E-I-O !

         D   **D**

With a cluck-cluck here, and a cluck-cluck there

[Continue with D]

Here a cluck, there a cluck, everywhere a cluck-cluck

       D   **G D**   **A7**   **D**

Old Mac Donald had a farm, E-I-E-I-O !

Row Row Row your Boat

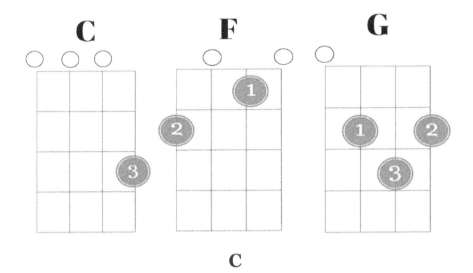

C

Row, row, row your boat

C

Gently down the stream.

F

Merrily, merrily, merrily, merrily,

G   **C**

Life is but a dream.

Frere Jacques

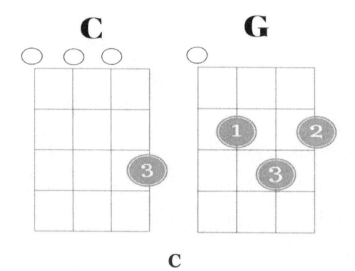

C

Frere Jacques, Frere Jacques

C

Dormez-vous, dormez-vous ?

C

Sonnez les matines, sonnez les matines,

G   **C**   **G**   **C**

Ding-dang-dong, ding-dang,dong

Hey Diddle Diddle

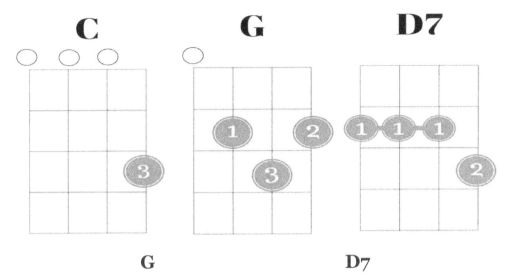

C　　　　**G**　　　　**D7**

　　　　　　　　　　G　　　　　　　　　　D7

Hey diddle diddle the Cat and the fiddle

　　　　　　　G　　　　　　　　　　D7

The cow jumped over the moon

　　　　　　　C　　　　　　　　　　G

The little dog laughed to see such sport

D7　　　　　　　　　　　　　　G

And the dish ran away with the spoon

The Alphabet Song

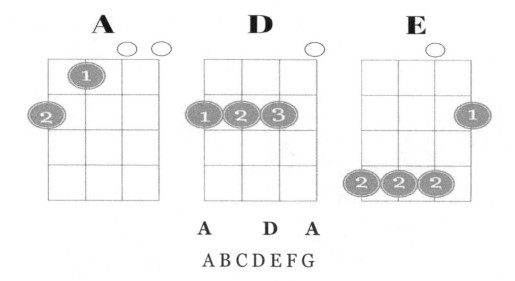

A   D   A

A B C D E F G

E A E   A

H I J K L M N O P

A   DA   E

Q R S T U V

A D A   E

W X Y and Z

A   D   A

Now I Know my A-B-Cs.

E   A   E   A

Next time won't you sing with me.

Kookaburra

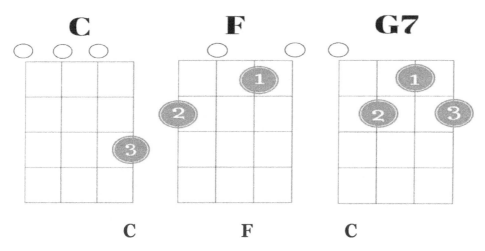

             C   F   C

Kookaburra sits in the old gum tree

          C   G7   C

Merry, merry king of the bush is he.

             F   C

Laugh, Kookaburra ! Laugh, Kookaburra !

                 C

Gay your life must be.

          C   G7   C

Eating all the gumdrops he can see.

             F   C

Stop, Kookaburra ! Stop, Kookaburra !

                 C

Leave some there for me !

Kumbaya

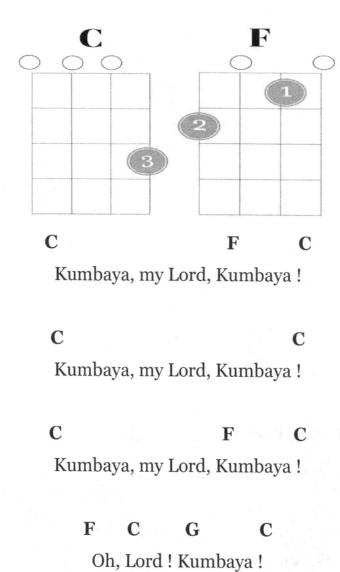

C   F   C

Kumbaya, my Lord, Kumbaya !

C   C

Kumbaya, my Lord, Kumbaya !

C   F   C

Kumbaya, my Lord, Kumbaya !

F   C   G   C

Oh, Lord ! Kumbaya !

This Little Light of Mine

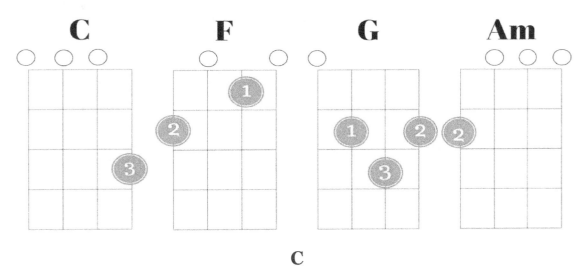

C

This little light of mine. I'm gonna let it shine.

F   C

This little light of mine. I'm gonna let it shine.

C   Am

This little light of mine. I'm gonna let it shine.

C   G   C

Let it shine, let it shine, let it shine.

Stand by-me

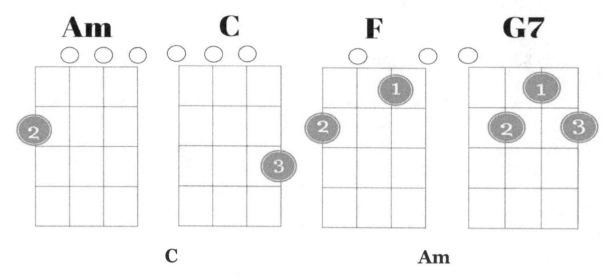

C   Am

When the night has come, and the land is dark and the

         F   G7   C

moon is the only light we see,

                   Am

Oh, I won't be afraid, no, I won't be afraid just as

        F   G7   C

Long as you stand, stand by me

Chorus

Am

So darlin , darlin, stand by me, oh stand by me, oh,

F   **G7**   **C**

Stand, stand by me, stand by me

C   **Am**

If the sky that we look upon, should tumble and fall and the

F   **G7**   **C**

mountains should crumble into the sea,

Am

I won't cry, I won't cry, no, I won't shed a tear just as

F   **G7**   **C**

long as you stand, stand by me

Repeat Chorus

   C   Am   F
Stand by me, oh stand by me, oh stand

      G7   C
Stand by me, stand by me. When ever I'm in trouble won't you

   C   Am   F
Stand by me, oh, stand by me, oh stand

      G7   C
Stand by me, stand by me. When ever I'm in trouble won't you

   C   Am   F
Stand by me, oh stand by me, oh stand

G7   C   C
Stand by me, stand by me, When ever I'm in trouble.

Conclusion

I truly hope this book on Ukulele beginner's instruction has been instrumental (pun intended) in guiding you on taking your first steps of a rewarding lifelong journey of musical enjoyment. I just want to share my love of this art with you! It truly is such a beautifully crafted instrument with a rich history.

Did you know that the ukulele has it's roots in Hawaii? However, that is not where it originated. In fact, it was first called the "machete de braga". The original style came from the Madeira Island near Portugal. They were brought to Hawaii by traveling merchants who were trading goods. Eventually the Hawaiians evolved the instrument into what it is today.

You can bet that whenever you are strumming away, playing the Ukulele, you will be transported to a world away. The music will land you right in Hawaii, with a lay around your neck and the warm sun at your back. Of course, the ukulele can only do this in your imagination. It certainly is not a portal to a tropical island!

As you read through this book, you became vastly more familiar with this carefree instrument. Let us try and recall what you should have taken away from this course: We learned how to choose a Ukulele from the available sizes and sample models and prices. The proper way to hold the Ukulele along with correct hand position and then tune it up. Then we progressed on to reading and understanding chords and their diagrams and a variety of strumming methods. You now should understand the different chord types e.g. Major, minor, 7ths and even a flat chord. Then you completed with some practice chord change exercises.

CPSIA information can be obtained
at www.ICGtesting.com
Printed in the USA
BVHW010819200421
605385BV00011B/175

9 781695 795907